Songlines

poems by

Meredith Heller

Finishing Line Press
Georgetown, Kentucky

Songlines

"Within the animist belief system of Indigenous Australians, a songline, also called dreaming track, is one of the paths across the land which mark the route."
~ Wikipedia

"Aboriginal creation myths tell of the legendary totemic being who wandered over the continent in the Dreamtime, singing out the name of everything that crossed their path—birds, animals, plants, rocks, waterholes—and so singing the world into existence.

The melodic contour of the song describes the land over which the song passes. A musical phrase is a map reference. Music is a memory bank for finding one's way about the world.

A Bushman child will be carried a distance of 4,900 miles before he begins to walk on his own. Since, during this rhythmic phase, he will be forever naming the contents of his territory, it is impossible he will not become a poet."
~ Bruce Chatwin, *The Songlines*

"Some people say poetry is the music of the written word."
~ Terry Clitheroe, *The Poet's Garret*

"A poem is a composition written for performance by human voice. What your eye sees on the page is the composers verbal score, waiting for your voice to bring it alive as you read it aloud or hear it in your mind's ear."
~ James Knapp

As a poet and singer/songwriter, a songline is a metaphor for how I map my way through the terrain of my life by writing poetry and music.
~ Meredith Heller, Big Sur, CA, April 2018

Copyright © 2019 by Meredith Heller
ISBN 978-1-63534-955-9 First Edition
All rights reserved under International and Pan-American Copyright Conventions. No part of this book may be reproduced in any manner whatsoever without written permission from the publisher, except in the case of brief quotations embodied in critical articles and reviews.

ACKNOWLEDGMENTS

For my mother, Peggy
For my father, Eugene
And for my spirit-mom, Annelies

Publisher: Leah Maines
Editor: Christen Kincaid
Cover Art: *Moon Faces* by Yzzy Demmon
Author Photo: Jesse Kincaid
Cover Design: Elizabeth Maines McCleavy

Printed in the USA on acid-free paper.
Order online: www.finishinglinepress.com
also available on amazon.com

Author inquiries and mail orders:
Finishing Line Press
P. O. Box 1626
Georgetown, Kentucky 40324
U. S. A.

Table of Contents

At Nine Years Old 1

Song of My Spine 2

I Wish You 4

For My Father 5

Passage of Light 7

How to Hum 8

A Name of My Own 9

Glenda 10

Like a Bird 12

This Blue Bowl 13

Fruitful Odes 15

Round Brown Stone 17

Ode to Blue 18

Leopard Sharks 19

Twenty Geese 20

Trust 21

Your Jacket 22

When a Man Is Blue 23

Clenched Fist 24

Grandma Esther 25

Joshua Tree 26

Breath 27

Georgia 30

Say Yes 31

Stories from Stones 33

At Nine Years Old

At nine years old, I rule the world
skipping through the grass
along the reflecting pool
in Washington, DC
on an impossibly humid day
in late August.

My mother leading the way
on one of her epic walkabouts
a bohemian cheerleader
in pigtails and bell-bottoms
tipsy on life
singing a song
only she knows.

And my sister
sulking behind us
overwrought and angry
fighting the world
for my mother's undivided attention
which none of us
will ever receive.

And I, elven-hearted and porous
dunk my head into the fountain
and hold my breath
until the world and the war and the heat
drain away.

And in that cool dark emptiness
a single thread of melody arises
and whispers itself into my left ear
like a vow.

I come up for air
whipping my hair
in an arc of splintered light
and I am humming
raw and incandescent.

Song of My Spine

I am this lithe spirit snake
rising up your back-body
like a sinuous river
singing my sensual songs.

I am this tall tree of spine
sending down my one strong root into the earth
and sending up my millions of tiny tendrils
which reach like fingers of light
into every part of your body
igniting you with life.

I am this neural freeway
that whirs with your every whim
anticipating the trajectory of your direction
sometimes before you even know where you're headed.

I am this electromagnetic lighthouse
that stands alone on my own precipice
sending out my signal to the world.

I am this cluster of fiber-optic threads
that weave their way through each of your limbs
like a symphonic telegraph
a nexus of light and sound
with sparks that speak across space as they orbit.

I am this bamboo flute
that sings with your every mood
I wail and hum
I sigh and shimmy
I bend in the wind.

At night, I curl myself up
into the dark soil of being
and each morning, I unfurl
a new green fiddlehead fern
raising my wild head to greet the day.

I am this supple segmented serpent
who climbs your back
housed in my white coral cathedral
backing up the choices of your heart.

I Wish You

I wish you mouthfuls of laughter and warm cozy hands and bowls of nourishing soup and starry-starry light glittering at the periphery of your eyes as if someone or something is tapping you gently on the shoulder, whispering a song from your childhood that makes you smile and weep at the same time, in a good way, like when you know who you are.

I wish you the scent of lime blossoms and the taste of salt on your lips and a silver feather tattooed across your belly, gentle and elusive as a water mark, and the inviting rhythm of rain on your roof that wakes you up at night and draws you from your bed to dance a little in the darkness with a prayer in your body.

I wish you a loving letter from an old friend when you least expect it, with words that warm you like small sticks of kindling that catch and smoke and smell of ancient sandalwood forests and the tiny blue birds that sing at night, unaware of the hour of their rapture, and a low slung moon, lying on her back, points up, like a bowl of light.

I wish you pan-fried plantains drizzled with honey and the lonely sound of a fog horn at dusk after it's rained all day, and the sweet, rich, gentleness you feel in every cell of your body when you're kind to another human being.

I wish you the stillness of the great blue heron and the way my heart grows wings when I see the sunlight spangle the water, and the feel of your back, leaning against these rocks here, that have soaked up the sun all day, humming their minerals into your bones, and this wide blue sky that touches the curves of the mountain tenderly with his hand and the way she arches up to meet him.

I wish you the cool clean whiteness of shells, the sacredness of bones, the memory of flight that leaves its signature in the feather. I wish you the wide wingspan of a low swooping owl as it turns ninety degrees on its side, to fly between trees in the forest, as you walk home alone one night, listening for your song.

For My Father ~ February 2017

When all the voices in my house
argued so loud
I couldn't hear myself sing,
I headed to the river.

When the knot in my belly
twisted so tight
I couldn't breathe,
I headed to the river.

When my mother huddled mouse-like in her corner
tapping the world with her magic wand
pretending that everything sparkled,
I headed to the river.

When my father retreated to his den
slamming the door
and drowning his depression in a bottle of gin,
I headed to the river.

The river, where the voices are clean and true
where the wind and water sing in harmony
where the gray granite rocks stand in stillness
and the great blue heron fishes from her perch
at the edge of the world.

And today,
this February full moon eclipse,
my father,
a tall, solid, solitary
oak of a man
fell in the forest.

But it was in witnessing
my father's passing
that I was woven into all that is holy
and given a new heart
that beats with fierce respect
for the great mystery
and cycle of life.

And for my father,
who finally became my friend,
who now meets me at the river
and lights around my shoulders
like a cloak of yellow butterflies
fluttering in the sun.

Passage of Light

Years after your anger boiled itself dry
scorching the vessel of your being clean

I came to understand
that we are the same animal

that our wounding bleeds the same color
only a different shade

and yours has left you, softer.
It has not disfigured you

sucking pain to your shoulders
like pins to magnet.

It has not gnawed through the nerve sheath
leaving you at its feral edge

like me,
where comfort knows no home

and my name changes
with the passage of light

How to Hum

Can you remember
how to whisper
to your heart
without crying?

Better yet, how to hum?

It was the high reach of your voice
that like a rope
you climbed

out of the knotted jungle
through the burnt lung
of night.

A Name of My Own

Tianna
It is a cracked tea cup
a gypsy reading tea leaves
pointing me Northwest
pushing me home.

My mother's name
and my mother's eyes
blue as glacial ice
cold as Alaska, alone.

Tianna is the cry
the seagull wails
as it fights
for a bite of bread.

It is the wish-bone
the wishing well
the wish I never made;
I will make it now
when no one is looking.

I wish for a name of my own

one that doesn't tinkle
in the glass
like ice-cubes

one that fills the house
with the smell of dried flowers
warmed on the stove

where my grandma
baked blackberry pie
and smoked cigarettes
before women were allowed.

Glenda

I was named after my grandpa Glen, and everybody just always called me Glen, that is until my baby brother Henry was born and then my daddy did me the justice of adding the "da" to the end of my name, to make it more feminine. I guess they really wanted a boy and once they got one, I could finally be a girl. But I never did hear the end of it because as soon as Henry could talk, he went running through the house, yelling at the top of his lungs: Glen-DUUHHH..., like he thought I was stupid or something, but I wasn't stupid, I just didn't feel much like talking. I already was talking, to God, and to the spirits of things.

Nothing much ever changes around here. There's nothing to do, except chores, and nowhere to go, except the river. I'm all growed up now, married with three kids of my own, and I'm only 21. My three boys are some kind of wild animals and I got another one cooking up here in my belly, as we speak. That's the way it is around here.

I've been kinda lonely since my sister, Caroline, took off for the big city to go be a model and all. She sure is pretty, but we don't see her much anymore. Oh, she sends postcards for our birthdays and I tape them up on the fridge, but I miss her. These days my best friend is Bessie the pig. I am hoping for a sweet baby girl this time who I will name Angelique and show her all the best swimming holes.

Jake, my husband, he's ok I guess. He works hard all day and comes home late and tired and wants dinner and a little pussy, but he always falls asleep before I cum, so I crawl off into the field behind our house, lie down in the grass, and pull my dress up around my waist, thinking I will touch myself, but more often than not, I just lose myself in the stars. In the morning, I wake up cold and run inside pretending I was just out collecting eggs for our breakfast. My oldest is the only one who notices. He's got his grandma's eyes, all sparkle and wise, like he knows things well beyond this Earth.

Sometimes I worry about my boys. I fear they will drown playing in that river the way they do. So once in a while I call them inside just to make sure they're ok. They get so mad at me and shoot me their evil-eye look, and I know what they're thinking, how dare you pull us away from our precious playtime. But my oldest, Orion, he'll come in and just sit with me real quiet like for awhile and then he smiles that smile of his and goes back out to join his brothers.

Jake's family is still upset with me. They wanted me to name my first born after Jake's father, but there was no way I was gonna name my boy after some old mean drunk, who never did nothing good for nobody. So instead, I named him after the constellation Orion, so that he will grow up a big strong warrior, whose only weapon is the light.

Like a Bird

Lyrics lift
from her lips
like a bird.

Turning ninety degrees on her side
one wing reaching
for the sun
one swooping low
hanging-five
stroking the water
with her feathered fingers.

She flies and she sings
of shadow and light
the rhythm of her tides
and the place
before either existed.

You see,
it's how she feels
when the wind
shivers the edge
of her wing

keeping her suspended

where everything and nothing
meld into one

leaving her breathless.

This Blue Bowl

This blue bowl
like an empty sky
turned inside out
with small fractures
where its earthen soul shows through
where its shine has been rubbed away
by stars passing through.

This blue bowl
turned on a wheel
turned in someone's hands
born of the gooey clay
that lay asleep inside the earth
holding her bones together.

This blue bowl
glazed with cerulean blue paint
made from glass that tumbled onto a tiny beach
in the Greek Islands by the Mediterranean Sea
where one day when I was 17,
I saw a man catch an octopus with his bare hands
and beat it against a rock until it was dead
and then take it home and cook it up
with garlic and onions,
leeks and tomatoes from his garden
and feed it to his wife and children
after a long day making blue glaze
under the hot sun.

This blue bowl
fired in the kiln
with fire from the sun
or wherever fire comes from;
where does fire live before it's born?

This blue bowl
held in the hands of every person
who helped make it
and bring it to market
where I bought it

and carried it home
in the basket on my bike.

This blue bowl
filled with dark purple grapes
the color of the night sky
when lightning cracks.

This blue bowl
that I hold in my hands
and pass into the hands of my beloved
who sits beside me munching grapes
and small pieces of dark chocolate
that he feeds me
with his fingers laughing
his mouth smiling
his eyes like river rocks
shining.

This blue bowl
like an empty sky
but not so empty
so very full
of all the hands
that shaped it

and now it holds its own palms open
up to the light.

Fruitful Odes

Orange

Who said you could be so round and bright like a beach ball?
Who said you could be so sweet and juicy inside
and pack a punch of Vitamin C?
Who said you could be the number one breakfast drink in the country?
Who said you could choose the boldest color in the rainbow
and claim its name as your own,
as if you didn't already command so much attention?
Who said you could grow in the hottest and most beautiful places on earth
and hang like glowing lanterns from the trees?

Banana

Yo, Banana!
You long, sleek thing, you.
You're the kayak that my friend Suzanni and I paddle down the river.
You're the hammock I take camping.
You're the crescent moon, slung low in the night sky.
You grow in groups like a family
hanging from the trees with the biggest leaves
so generous of you to offer shade and a snack on a hot summer day.
You're famous for being split and cradling ice cream in a dish,
but I like to peel you and freeze you,
just as you are
you're the star in my morning smoothie.

Mango

Mama Mango
Heart of fire
You rolled through the sunset and stole all its colors to paint your skin.
I first met you in my grandpa's garden,
hanging from the trees like great big birthday balloons;
I didn't know you were so sweet until I went to the islands.
I had only tasted you in my grandma's jam,
bitter with lemon rind and apricot pits.
But you, my creamy queen of the islands,

you, are my ambrosia.

Strawberry

Hey cutie, do you know you have your dress on inside out?
Do you know you're the only fruit to wear its seeds on the outside?
Is this safe?
And on the inside, where your seeds should be,
there is a tiny hollow pocket, shaped like a heart.
Do you have room in your heart for me?

Round Brown Stone

Round brown stone
you were born in the painted mountains
behind my mother's house
under a sea blue sky.

When you were four
you had a birthday party
and you learned how to roll
you've been rolling ever since.

At seven you packed a small bag
kissed your mom and dad goodbye
and tumbled down the hill.

You negotiated your way between trees
stopping occasionally
for a slow dip
in a cool stream.

At nine you met a frog
and learned how to jump
you've been jumping ever since.

At eleven you jumped into my hand
while I was walking through the woods
you were warm and smooth
you smelled like iron
you smelled like the wind.

I wanted to put you in my pocket
and take you home with me
but I sensed that you wanted to keep moving.

So I returned you gently
to the earth
where there was a view
of the trees and sky.

And I walked home knowing
you had taught me about freedom.

Ode to Blue

Blue is my favorite t-shirt when I was a kid
aqua blue, with three-quarter sleeves
the softest cotton
from being washed and worn so many times.

Two white stripes circle each upper arm
I am a Native American
and these stripes, my war paint
when I wear this shirt, I am invincible.

Blue bike for my birthday
with banana seat and high handle bars
my blue horse.
I ride him every day after school
on the street behind my house
my brown mane flying in the wind.

Blue is the sky that connects the whole world
all the other kids on all the other continents
looking up right now into that blue
and wondering what else is out there.

Blue are the birds that sing
the song of late afternoon
as they gather worms with blue bellies for their dinner
their nests woven with strands of blue ribbon
pecked from the trash.

Blue is my blood when it's inside my skin
until I take the last turn too fast
and scrape my knee.
Blue is the band-aid that seals my wound
with a kiss from my mother's lips.

Blue is my mood
when she says it's too late to go back out and play
but the moon is full, Mom,
it's calling my name.

Leopard Sharks

    Listen,

today there were leopard sharks
    in Richardson's Bay

        hundreds of them
            galloping
                and turning
                    through the water.

    It was thrilling.

I wanted to get into the water with them
        not as me
           but as one of them

                sliding
                    on angles of light

    their spotted bodies

            slicing

                through the dark unknown.

Twenty Geese
Memorial for a Boyfriend's Father

This morning, as I walked along Richardson's Bay, a flock of twenty geese, turned their long white bodies toward the sun and glided as one being across the sky.

They dipped and saluted, revealing the black underbelly of their wings, like the stripes of a captain.

Moving effortlessly like tides, they ebbed and flowed in and out of V-formation, painting the sky with clean strokes of white each time they changed direction.

They flew over my head and over the house, where today, at 2pm, we will hold your father's memorial. I wanted to join their dance. I imagined my fingertips brushing their wingtips, the freedom of air, and me, joining that one-body they all comprised.

I watched them for about twenty minutes, it seemed like a very long time, not that they were counting, not by my clock anyway. No, they exist only in the moment, the only tug of time, the change of season calling them South. And I thought about your father, sailing from New Zealand to the United States, meeting your mother and raising a family with triplets, one of whom is you, while building his get-away boat in the backyard. Then like the geese, he felt the call and he sailed South, back to New Zealand.

And I thought about your father, and releasing his ashes today into the bay at Mermaid Point, his scattered ashes which will lift and blow in the wind and look much like this flock of birds that floats above me now.

And I made a promise to watch as each particle that was your father, rises and glitters in the light for one infinitesimal moment before disappearing into the great mystery.

I thought about the invisible net that connects the whole universe and holds us all to it, until eventually, it releases us.

And I thought, this is it, each moment, each life, unique and shimmering, connected and shifting between being separate and being part of the whole, and how the time we get here is just so brief before we fly off into our final migration.

Trust

If you say the word trust to yourself
five times fast
do you start to believe it?

If you suck on it
like a butterscotch candy
your grandpa gave you
does it get sweeter to swallow?

If you squeeze it in your hands
as tight as you can
then open them quickly
as if setting something free
does it make it easier to understand
that trust is not about holding on
but about letting go?

And when you sit up alone at 3am,
gnawing on the bone of your heart
dreading that the one you love
is loving someone else,
make yourself remember
that trust is not about whether another person loves you
but rather about knowing your own self worth
all the way down to your bones,

and that it is not about whether another person is true to you
but rather that you are true to the vows you've taken
for your own happiness and theirs.

And when the geese fly south for the winter, in pairs,
honking in harmony mid-flight,
do you get that if two souls truly lift each other up,
they will keep choosing to be together
because they make each other sing?

Your Jacket

You're asking me to take off
the musky velvet of your skin
like a worn and cherished jacket
and fold it neatly
along the original creases
that I no longer remember
because they don't include me.

In the great green bounding
stride of your youth
it is remarkable
that you paused
to wind the wiry sap of your body
around my weathered soul.

If I return to you
your jacket
that once held me
in its pocket
like a lucky stone
would you give me
just a moment
to slip my arms
into the long sleeves of sadness
that wrap your memory around me
tight as my breath.

My fingers wrestle the buttons
seeking closure
but you won't let me
near enough
to say goodbye.

So I leave the jacket open
hanging loosely at my hip
and swinging
on a creaky hinge.

When a Man Is Blue

The hollow of his chest
is a dark place
        where loneliness grows.

Each breath cracks a rib
collapses a lung
        swallows the incoming light.

Every morning he walks to his bench
on two strong legs
        wears holes in the day with his thoughts.

Every evening he returns home
a crumpled brown paper bag
        folds himself into the night.

Clenched Fist

My head is lead.
My body stone.

My blood icy-hot
scratching
as it moves
through my veins.

My lips
that once kissed you
are now split and bleeding
dried-up crones,

too bitter
to even
gossip.

My body is
a clenched
fist.

Grandma Esther

Your body is a rundown tenement
broken bricks your back
fractured windows your eyes
ravaged beams your bones,
yet you stand
a monument.

The five senses of your walls
have withstood the constant thrum
of your heart
slumped inward on itself,
beating a bitter dirge.

So what holds the soul
of your house together
old woman?

Threadbare and sutured
your frown holds like a scar
bolted across the door of your face.

Shut in and shut out
Grandma, it's me:
LET-ME-IN!

89 years you march
waving your flag for martyrdom,
I will not follow you.

Joshua Tree

I have been shivering
since the desert welcomed us
with fingers of ice.

I have crawled
into the cave
of my body

and I'm not coming out

until the breakfast of springtime

when the heart breaks open

like an egg.

Breath

It was I,
who first swept across the desert
scattering ashes from the explosion
blowing seeds into tiny crevices of rock
that in a billion years would gather water
and sprout life.

I connect all things and all people
separation is illusion.

In the dance between molecules
I heat up
I cool down.

It is I,
passing through space
who bumps and rubs
against matter as I go
howling
        moaning
                strumming the marimba.

I balance an easy orbit
between the bowl of your sacrum
and the globe of your skull.

Often I race into you and stop short
often you don't even notice
        when I've wandered out.

Sometimes you gasp as you take me in
grunt as you let me out
      pant
          sigh
                bellow at my breast.

Yet, always, I am here
waiting for you
to remember me.

I am the one,
with my hand curled like a fetus
around the spiral shell of your ear

    whispering incantations
           love songs
                    lullabies
                            prayers.

I am the one,
licking your lips as you sing
when you weave miraculous tales
        when you scream fire from your belly
                when you sob slow blue tears.

When we walk hand in hand
we are the Cirque de Soleil
    the aurora borealis
        Gershwin's Rhapsody in Blue.

When you love with others
I kneel before the harmony of your chorus.
In quiet moments
we are one voice singing with God.

When I fill you
and you shudder.
When I slip the barrier
of your skin and flesh,
to taste the spaces
of your emptiness.

I am the one,
reaching out
to the thin skin of balloon
that holds you tethered.

I am the one,
    climbing out to your edge
until I boomerang back.

Deflated.

I am made to surrender everything,
all I have just gathered in my greedy arms
I dump at your feet.

    Your summer gardens
            your rain-fed fountains
                  your sun-scorched stones
                        your apricot mornings
                              your long daytime strides

Your ragged nights
        your mystic rivers
                your motes
                        your labyrinths
                              your Celtic knots,

I have dwelt in them all.

I am your faithful companion.

You have held me
in all your canyons and reservoirs
taking me with you
        wherever you go
                without ever having to think.

You have always done
what is most natural,
        to take me in
                to let me go.

Still, I am
always waiting
for that rare moment
when you allow me
to hold you.

In the end, I have only offerings.
I ask nothing and want nothing.
I am empty and free
with no story and no dream.

If another wave picks me up
and rolls me through your body
then I sing reborn,
        if not,
                I rest
                        resolved.

Georgia

Ghost Ranch
Abiquiú
sun baked day

cracking
      the earth and sky
             open.

Oh, to be Georgia O'Keefe
painting vagina-flowers
in the 1930's
      in the desert

with Alfred Stieglitz
      watching
             from behind the lens.

He, capturing a single moment
      of her ever-changing spirit.

His own feelings
      snapping
             open and shut.

Their connection
      an aperture
             of blossoming light.

Georgia and Ansel Adams,
a study of relationship
      between form and space

the verity of black and white
      the sensuality of the natural world
             the infinite palette of gray.

Yosemite at dawn.
Yosemite at dusk.

Georgia,
under a full moon
      dancing with the wind.

Say Yes

At midnight on Tuesday
her flower bloomed
beside the Yuba River
that pours in pulses of lace
through the eye holes
of the rock skulls
that rest their heads
on the bank
to dream.

She cracks and crumbles
into the murmur of water
that signs its name across her skin
delicately devouring her edges
until even the essence of her soul
dissolves.

The granite boulders of her back
marbled with grief
break apart at the seams
scatter the water with sparks
from her veins.

Say yes to an invitation from Hades
received on a handwritten scroll
tied with a white string
hidden in a rock crevice
and read one evening
as the moon sliced the sky.

Now jasmine flowers bloom in her hair
sage roots through her toes,
she remembers when kids played kickball
on the street behind her house
one humid summer night

when she stayed out late
with the boy who read a book
under the street lamp
while bats darted in and out

catching moths in their mouths.

Language was a song she sang
as she rode her bike
up and down the hill
a melody tattooed its signature
across her shoulders
in notes she bent
on the lute of her ribs,
her polkadot shirt unbuttoned
flying in the breeze behind her
her heart open to the sun.

Resist resistance
she sings to herself
like a mantra.

The supple sapling of her spine
rises toward the light
as she spins on a tilted axis
from gravity's hip.

The water takes and turns her
in its wise white hands
as she composts last year's loss.

In the morning
a velvet peach ripens in her throat
she warbles as she's born.

Year after year
of dark nights
and bright noon-tides,
the zippered pocket
of her being
opens
and closes.

Stories from Stones

Day 1:
The river glowed today
her face freckled with sun.
She hummed and bubbled
with a new song.
She etched her name
in circles on the rocks.
She laid her bare belly across their backs
and they drank the sorrow from her bones.

What's underneath all the sadness?
What pulls everything into this dark eddy?
She touches the sadness with her finger
and peels it away
layer after layer
until she finds a young child
sitting alone on a rock
a full moon rising in her face
starfish growing in her hands
her heart, longing for love.

She teaches the child
how to sing to the music of the river
how to listen to the stories from stones.
She shows her how to place her hand on her heart
and pledge her love to life.

The wind blows through the child's hair
each tendril turns into a striped snake
that sings in its own language.

Crickets gossip.
The sky turns to smoke
and slips into the water like a fish.
It weaves a cord of copper rope.
The child catches it
and spins like a dervish.

The first star sparks the sky with flint.
She breathes its white fire into her belly.

Bats swoop in jagged angles above her head.
The rocks lift their wizened faces to the sky
their eyes glinting with gold.

She eats her evening meal
with a spoon carved from oak
its dark tongue quenching her.

The moon sleeps
curled on her side
her light spilling over.

A night bird calls her name
as she crawls into her feathered nest
the water full of jade.

Day 2:
It's after midnight
when they finally climb across the rock
into each other's bodies.
Between them grows a creature with wings
that glow iridescent like an opal
in the moonlight.
The creature catches a falling star
on the tip of its tongue.

They make a nest
beside the granite rocks
and she wraps her filigree fronds
around his trunk.
They sleep beneath the eyes of the stars
while the water creature
mumbles prayers
into their ears.

Day 3:
Morning wakes them
by strumming a few chords of color across the sky.
Tall pines breathe above them.
The river roars with joy.

She watches her friend slink up the canyon
leaving her in the bright hands of morning.

She swims in the river.
The sun drinks water droplets from her skin
like a child licking an ice cream cone.

She melts into the granite boulder
that holds her against its body
like a lover.

Just me and the river, she thinks,
the air humming with dragonflies,
the only words left in her mouth are:
Thank You.

Day 4:
All night and all morning
the river and I flow downstream
sharing love songs.

Under the water the stones gather
in patterns of sacred geometry
pushed and pulled
by the magnetics of their minerals
aligning along invisible threads
that hum with life.

Yuba River, your veins filled with gold
you lick me with your mossy tongue
your own skin rippling
as I lose my edges
dissolve into the sun
and come out the other side.

Meredith Heller is a poet and singer/songwriter with graduate degrees in writing and education. A California Poet in the Schools, she teaches poetry & creative writing, coaches private voice & songwriting, leads *Moontribe* 'Write of Passage' Nature Program for teen girls, and hosts *Siren Song*, a women's singer/songwriter night. Her poetry has been published in *Rebelle Society, We'Moon, Quiet Lightning, The Aquarian, Avocet,* and in *Women, Their Names, & The Stories They Tell*. Her essays appear in *Common Ground* and *Tiny House Magazines*. A nature-girl who spent fifteen summers solo backpacking, she hikes the trails daily and lives in a tiny cottage made from a train caboose in Marin County, California. She is mused by nature, synchronicity, and kindred souls.

Visit her blog: www.BonesofSynchronicity.com

www.ingramcontent.com/pod-product-compliance
Lightning Source LLC
LaVergne TN
LVHW050045090426
835510LV00043B/3209